Rectangle Ranch

written by **Molly Dingles**
illustrated by **Len Dobson**

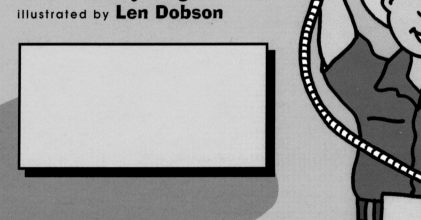

dingles & company New Jersey

For Tracey

First printing

PUBLISHED BY dingles&company

P.O. Box 508 • Sea Girt, New Jersey • 08750
WEBSITE: www.dingles.com • E-MAIL: info@dingles.com

LIBRARY OF CONGRESS CATALOG CARD NO.: 2004095734
ISBN: 1-59646-035-0

Printed in the United States of America

ART DIRECTION & DESIGN BY Barbie Lambert
EDITED BY Andrea Curley
EDUCATIONAL CONSULTANT Maura Ruane McKenna
ART ASSISTANT Erin Collity
PRE-PRESS BY Pixel Graphics

Molly Dingles is the author of *Jinka Jinka Jelly Bean* and *Little Lee Lee's Birthday Bang*, as well as the Community of Color and the Community of Counting series. She is a writer and lyricist who holds a bachelor's degree in fine arts/theater from Mount Saint Mary's College and a master's degree in educational theater from New York University. She lives in Manasquan, New Jersey, with her husband, David.

Len Dobson is a graphic designer and illustrator. He has a national degree in graphic design from Guildford School of Art. His interest in children's books stems from the ten years he worked with BBC Worldwide and Warner Bros. to create cartoon characters for merchandising in the gift industry. Len has enjoyed a good deal of success in his professional career, and has since pursued his ambitions in publishing.

The Community of Shapes series is more than just a series of books about shape identification. The series demonstrates how individual people, places, and things combine to form a community. It allows children to view the world in segments and then experience the wonderment and value of the community as a whole.

What is a Rectangle?

Technical definition:

A four-sided figure with four right angles and adjacent sides of unequal length.

Kid-friendly definition:

A four-sided figure with two longer sides and two shorter sides.

Rectangle
ranch sign

Rectangle
bales of hay

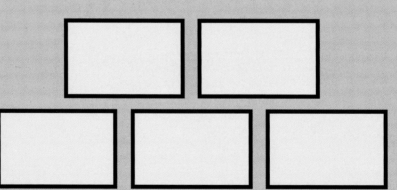

Rectangle
belt buckle

Rectangle
bricks of clay.

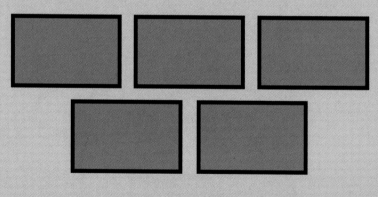

Rectangle
stable doors

Rectangle
bin for feed

Rectangle
barn windows

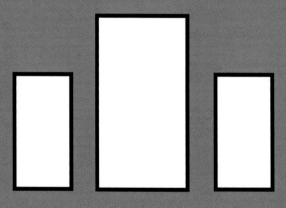
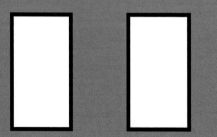

Rectangle
box for seed.

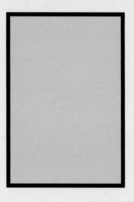

Rectangle
welcome flag

Rectangle
cattle brand

Rectangle
fence railings

Rectangle planter stand.

Rectangle shapes are all around.

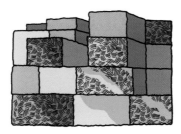

Where on this ranch can they be found?

ABOUT SHAPES

Use the Community of Shapes series to teach your child to identify the most basic shapes and to help him or her relate these shapes to objects in the real world. ASK:

- What shape is this book about?
- How many rectangular windows are on the big barn?
- Can you identify the biggest rectangle in each picture? The smallest?
- What is your favorite rectangular-shaped object? Why?

ABOUT COMMUNITY

Use the Community of Shapes series to teach your child how he or she is an important part of the community. EXPLAIN TO YOUR CHILD WHAT A COMMUNITY IS.

- A community is a place where people live, work, and play together.
- Your family is a community.
- Your school is a community.
- Your neighborhood is a community.
- The world is one big community.

Everyone plays an important part in making a community work – moms, dads, boys, girls, police officers, firefighters, teachers, mail carriers, garbage collectors, store clerks, and even animals are all important parts of a community. USE THESE QUESTIONS TO FURTHER THE CONVERSATION:

- How are the children interacting with one another at the ranch?
- How are the people different from one another? How are they the same?
- What do they have in common?
- How is the community you see in this book like your community? How is it different?
- Describe your community.

OBSERVATIONS

The Community of Shapes series can be used to sharpen your child's awareness of the shapes of objects in their surroundings. Encourage your child to look around and tell you what he or she sees. ASK:

- Can you find rectangle shapes in your house?
- Can you find rectangle shapes outside of your house?
- What rectangular-shaped object do you use most often?

TRY SOMETHING NEW ... Collect boxes of dog or cat food from your family and friends. Then donate them to your local animal shelter!